THE ALIENS HAVE LANDED!

THE ALIENS HAVE LANDED!

Poems by Kenn Nesbitt

Illustrations by Margeaux Lucas

Meadowbrook Press

Distributed by Simon & Schuster
New York

Library of Congress Cataloging-in-Publication Data

Nesbitt, Kenn.
    The aliens have landed! : poems / by Kenn Nesbitt.
        p. cm.
    ISBN 0-88166-396-4 (Meadowbrook) ISBN 0-689-84708-4 (Simon & Schuster)
    1. Children's poetry, American. [1. American poetry. 2. Humorous poetry.] I. Title.
PS3614.E47 A79 2001
811'.54—dc21   00-069575

Editorial Director: Christine Zuchora-Walske
Editor: Bruce Lansky
Coordinating Editor and Copyeditor: Angela Wiechmann
Proofreader: Megan McGinnis
Production Manager: Paul Woods
Desktop Publishing: Danielle White
Illustrations: Margeaux Lucas

© 2001 by Kenn Nesbitt
/0009

Published by Meadowbrook Press, 5451 Smetana Drive, Minnetonka, MN 55343

www.meadowbrookpress.com / www.gigglepoetry.com / www.kennnesbitt.com

BOOK TRADE DISTRIBUTION by Simon & Schuster, a division of Simon and Schuster, Inc., 1230 Avenue of the Americas, New York, NY 10020

05 04 03 02 01   10 9 8 7 6 5 4 3 2 1

Printed in the United States of America

Dedication

For Ann, Max, and Madison

Acknowledgments

Most of all, thank you, Ann, for teaching me that writing poetry is the most important work I do and for encouraging me to write this book. Thank you, Mom and Dad, for giving me a love of poetry as a child. Thank you to my editors, Bruce Lansky and Angie Wiechmann, for believing in this book and working so hard to make it as good as possible. Thank you, Linda Knaus, for your valuable feedback, your boundless sense of humor, and your amazing poetry. And thank you, Jack Prelutsky, for writing such wonderful books and inspiring children and children's poets everywhere.

Many thanks to the following teachers and their students:

Marcy Anderson, Dell Rapids Elementary, Dell Rapids, SD; Kate Arthurs, St. Martin's Episcopal School, Metairie, LA; Patty Bachman, Rockford, IL; Karen Benson, Highland Elementary, Apple Valley, MN; Mark Benthall, Austin, TX; Kathy Budahl, L. B. Williams Elementary, Mitchell, SD; Bonnie Cox, Kolmar School, Midlothian, IL; Cheryl Esparza, Monroe School, Hinsdale, IL; Linda Evans, Longfellow School, Sioux Falls, SD; Nancie Gordon, Whispering Pines Elementary, Miami, FL; Jane Hesslein, Sunset Hill Elementary, Plymouth, MN; Kelly Hinds, Simmons Elementary, Aberdeen, SD; Kate Hooper, Island Lake Elementary, Shoreview, MN; Angela Jalonack-Farnsworth, St. Paul, MN; Ann Johnson, McAuliffe Elementary, Hastings, MN; Sharon Klein, Clardy Elementary, Kansas City, MO; Barbara Knoss, Hanover School, Hanover, MN; Maggie Knutson, Orono Intermediate School, North Long Lake, MN; Carol Larson, Mississippi Elementary, Coon Rapids, MN; Karolyn Lee, Bloomington, MN; Julie Meissner, Turtle Bay School, Redding, CA; Karen Mink, Edgewood School, Woodridge, IL; Jenny Myer, New Richmond, WI; Elaine Nick, Gracemor Elementary, Kansas City, MO; Tessie Oconer, Fulton Elementary, Minneapolis, MN; Eric Ode, Stewart Elementary, Puyallup, WA; Connie Parrish, Gertie Bell Rodgers Elementary, Mitchell, SD; Mitzi Pearlman, Acres Green Elementary, Littleton, CO; Robert Pottle, Franklin, ME; John Pundsack, New Richmond, WI; Maria Jane Savaiano, Museum Magnet School, St. Paul, MN; Maria Smith, Bass Race Elementary, Crowley, TX; Tim Tocher, George Grant Mason Elementary, Tuxedo, NY; Lynette Townsend, Lomarena Elementary, Laguna Hills, CA; Julie White, New Richmond, WI; Sue Wiechmann, Riverside Elementary, Brainerd, MN; DeLinda Youngblood, Centralia, IL.

Contents

The Aliens Have Landed!

The aliens have landed!
It's distressing, but they're here.
They piloted their flying saucer
through our atmosphere.

2

They landed like a meteor
engulfed in smoke and flame.
Then out they climbed immersed in slime
and burbled as they came.

Their hands are greasy tentacles.
Their heads are weird machines.
Their bodies look like cauliflower
and smell like dead sardines.

Their blood is liquid helium.
Their eyes are made of granite.
Their breath exudes the stench of foods
from some unearthly planet.

And if you want to see these
sickly, unattractive creatures,
you'll find them working in your school;
they all got jobs as teachers.

Mithing Tooth

I'm having trouble thpeaking
thinthe I lotht my middle tooth.
Jutht yethterday my tooth wath fine—
today it wiggled loothe.

At firtht I thought it thilly
when my tooth fell out today,
but no one theemth to underthtand
a thingle word I thay.

I athked my mom to clothe the door.
She thaid, "That would be rude.
The door does not like wearing clothes;
it's happy in the nude."

I thaid a mouthe wath in my room
and she should come and thee.
She thaid, "Your mouth is on your face;
it's right where it should be."

I wonder if you underthtand
the thircumthtanthe I'm in.
I told her I wath feeling thick.
She thaid, "You're looking thin."

At latht she thaw how mad I wath
and thought I might thtop breathing.
She laughed and thaid she didn't mean it—
she wath only teething.

Mashed Potatoes on the Ceiling

Mashed potatoes on the ceiling.
Green beans on the floor.
Stewed tomatoes in the corner.
Squash upon the door.

Pickled peppers in my pocket.
Spinach up my sleeves.
Mushrooms in my underpants with
leeks and lettuce leaves.

Okra, onions, artichokes,
asparagus, and beets
buried neatly underneath the
cushions of our seats.

All the rest I've hidden in my socks
and down my shirt.
I'm done with all my vegetables.
I'm ready for dessert!

How Not to Play with Your Food

Don't play baseball with your Brussels sprouts
or tennis with tomatoes.
Don't play soccer with your succotash
or Ping-Pong with potatoes.

Don't play hockey with your hot dogs.
Don't go bowling with your beans.
Don't play racquetball with rump roast.
Don't play tag with tangerines.

When you're sitting at the table,
just enjoy your mother's cooking
and refrain from playing with your food—
except when no one's looking.

7

Abusement Park

We went to an amusement park,
my family and I.
We rode on rides so scary,
I expected I would die.

We rode a roller coaster
called The Homicidal Comet.
It had so many loop-de-loops
it nearly made us vomit.

We rode The Crazed Tornado,
and it jerked us hard and quick.
If it were any longer,
we would certainly be sick.

We rode The Psycho Octopus,
which packed a nasty punch.
I think we're pretty lucky
that we didn't lose our lunch.

And last we rode repeatedly
The Flailing Tilt-a-Whirl.
It shook us all so sharply,
I'm surprised we didn't hurl.

I haven't felt that nauseous
since I can't remember when.
I'm really looking forward
to the day we go again.

Kangaroos

If a person has four babies,
you would call them all quadruplets.
If a kangaroo does likewise,
should you call them kangaruplets?

And there's something else I wonder
that could use illuminating:
When a kangaroo is thinking,
is it kangaruminating?

If you baked a kangaroo a pie
and shaped it like a boomerang,
would it be best with whipping cream
or maybe kangaroo meringue?

I've got so many questions,
I just don't know what to do.
I guess perhaps I'll have to go
and ask a kangaroo.

The Skunk and the Porcupine

A skunk fell in love with a porcupine;
they married and had a baby.
I think that they called it a skunkupine,
or was it a porcuskunk, maybe?

Perhaps it was really a punkuskine,
or maybe a pinyskorkpunk.
There's only one thing that's for certain—
it felt like a cactus and stunk.

11

Springy Sidewalk

The people outside on the sidewalk
can't seem to remain on the ground.
They're jumping and hopping and springing
and generally bouncing around.

I've never seen anything like it.
It's quite an unusual scene,
as if they have springs in their sneakers
or bounce on a big trampoline.

I think I know what may have happened
to cause this chaotic event:
Last week they replaced our old sidewalk
with one made of rubber cement.

Nicknames

My aunt calls me "Elizabeth."
My grandma calls me "Liz."
My sister calls me "Lisa,"
and the baby calls me "Wiz."

My uncle calls me "Betty,"
while my grandpa calls me "Beth."
My brother calls me "Dizzy Liz"
or sometimes "Lizard Breath."

My teacher calls me "Betsy,"
and my friends all call me "Bess."
I find these nicknames more annoying
than you'd ever guess.

I wish that they would call me
by my real name instead.
I simply *hate* those nicknames;
see, my real name is Fred.

My Feet

My feet, my feet,
I love my feet.
I think they're great.
I think they're neat.
They're pretty, pink,
and picturesque.
They look so perfect
on my desk.
Unfortunately,
sad to tell,

they also have
a funny smell.
So though I'm fast,
and though I'm fleet,
and though at sports
I can't be beat,
no team will pick
me to compete
because they always
smell defeat.

15

I Stuck My Finger up My Nose

I stuck my finger up my nose
to see what it contained.
I found a bunch of crazy things
that cannot be explained.

I found a dozen rubber bands.
I found a piece of string.
I found my missing basketball.
I found a playground swing.

I found a giant pot of gold.
I found a sailing boat.
I found an ancient castle
with a drawbridge and a moat.

I found a hairy mastodon.
I found a purple car.
I found an Earth-bound starship
from a not-too-distant star.

But now despite the awesome stuff
I found inside my snout,
I wish I'd never poked in there—
my finger won't come out!

At Standing Still I Have a Skill

At standing still I have a skill
that truly is unique.
At sleeping I'm unquestionably
on a winning streak.

At lying down I'm unsurpassed;
I'm simply undefeated.
At sitting I'm the reigning champ;
I'll never be unseated.

At drifting in a daydream
it is obvious I'm blessed.
At staring at the TV
I'm undoubtedly the best.

At doing nothing
I am even better than you'd think.
At everything besides that, though,
I'd have to say I stink.

I hope someday I'll maybe learn
another kind of skill.
Until then I'm content to be
the best at standing still.

18

The Creatures of Bleen

The creatures of Bleen
are uncommonly clean;
they're exceedingly tidy and neat.
They have sponges and mops
on their bottoms and tops.
They have brooms on their hands and their feet.

The creatures of Bleen
can be frequently seen
on a scrubbing and straightening spree.
Every morning at nine
they wipe, launder, and shine
every last bit of trash and debris.

The creatures of Bleen
make a sparkling scene
as they gleefully clean up their rooms.
Then precisely at two
they use soap and shampoo
as they wash all their brushes and brooms.

The creatures of Bleen
have a shimmering sheen
as they're dusting their dressers and shelves.
For they finish each day
in the most bizarre way,
when they sit down and polish themselves.

19

I Love Me

I took myself out on a date
and said I'm looking grand,
and when I got my courage up,
I asked to hold my hand.

I took me to a restaurant
and then a movie show.
I put my arm around me
in the most secluded row.

I whispered sweetly in my ear
of happiness and bliss,
and then I almost slapped me
when I tried to steal a kiss.

Then afterwards I walked me home,
and since I'm so polite,
I thanked me for a perfect date
and wished myself good-night.

There's just one little problem,
and it kind of hurts my pride:
Myself would not invite me in,
so now I'm locked outside!

Pelican

A pelican fly and a pelican swing
and a pelican bounce on your bed.
And a pelican dance and a pelican sing
and a pelican stand on his head.

A pelican paddle a pelicanoe,
and a pelican pilot a yacht.
There are so many things that a pelican do,
but there's not much a pelicannot.

I Left Our Rhino in the Rain

I left our rhino in the rain;
all night he's been outside.
The rain has soaked him to the bone,
right through his rhino hide.

He's my responsibility.
My folks said, "Don't forget..."
But somehow I neglected him,
and now he's soaking wet.

And both my folks are all upset
and feel I can't be trusted.
I left our rhino in the rain,
and he rhinocerusted.

My Senses All Are Backward

My senses all are backward,
and it really makes me wonder
if on the day that I was born
somebody made a blunder.

For, strange but true, my senses
all got totally reversed.
Now everything I like the best
is what you'd call the worst.

I only like the smell of things
that frighten other noses.
I love the odor of a skunk.
I hate the smell of roses.

I only like the taste of foods
that cause most folks to shiver.
I hate the taste of chocolate.
I'm crazy over liver.

I'm not too fond of music,
but there's simply no denying
I like the sound of honking horns
and little babies crying.

I hate the feel of silky, velvet
softness on my skin.
I much prefer the sting I get
from sitting on a pin.

I hate the look of anything
that's really cute and snuggly.
The things I think are pretty
are what most consider ugly.

So let me tell you one more thing
before I have to go:
I think you are the most attractive
person that I know.

Ancient

He's older than the oldest man
that anyone has ever known.
He's older than the Internet;
he's older than the telephone.
He's older than the printed word,
the ancient Greeks, the dodo bird.
He's older than the pyramids
and prehistoric hominids.
He's older than the dinosaurs,
the earth, the sun, the moon, and stars.
He's old as mud, he's old as dust;
he's wrinkled up and turned to rust.
He's musty, crusty, stinky, dirty.
Simply put: Dad's turning thirty.

Mrs. DeBuss

Our second grade teacher, named Mrs. DeBuss,
has never had such a fun classroom as us.
You see, all the students have interesting names
instead of just plain ones, like Sarah or James.

So when she calls roll it is terribly funny;
she calls "Lauren Order" and then "Xavier Money."
Then "Ben Dare" and "Dawn Datt" and "Isabel Ringing,"
"Amanda B. Reckondwith," "Ella Fantsinging."

She calls "Cole Doubtside," "Anna Won," "Anna Tu,"
"Justin Time," "Justin Case," "Ahmal Wright," "Howard Yu."
She calls "Noah Liddle" and "Isaiah Lott"
plus "Diane Tumeechu" and "Heywood U. Knott."

"Claire Skyes" and "Paige Turner" and "Mike Carson-Fire."
"Jack Hammer," "Paul Barer," "Ed Hertz," and "Barb Dwyer."
Then "Colin Alcars," "Moira Less," and "Les Moore,"
"Sonny Day," "Sandy Beach," and then "Robin D. Store."

She calls "Woody Dewitt" and "I. Betty Wood,"
"Jose Ken Yusee" and then "Willie B. Goode."
She calls "Marcus Downe" and then "Natalie Drest,"
and lastly, of course, she calls "Olive D. Wrest."

Mrs. DeBuss

Advice from Dracula

Don't ever dine with Frankenstein;
he feasts on flaming turpentine.
He chomps and chews on soles of shoes
and quaffs down quarts of oily ooze.
At suppertime he'll slurp some slime.
He's known to gnaw on gristly grime.
His meals of mud and crispy crud
will curl your hair and chill your blood.
His poison, pungent, putrid snacks
may cause you seizures and attacks.
Your hair may turn completely white.
You may pass out or scream in fright.

Your skin will crawl.
Your throat will burn.
Your eyes will bulge.
Your guts will churn.
Your teeth will clench.
Your knees will shake.
Your hands will sweat.
Your brain will bake.
You'll cringe and cry.
You'll moan and whine.
You'll feel a chill
run down your spine.
You'll lose your lunch.
You'll lose your head.
So come...
and dine with *me* instead.

The Shower Is Running

My sister left the shower running
just the other day.
We had to chase it down the street;
it nearly got away.
Today the sink was running,
and it ran right out the door.
My sister's not allowed to touch
the faucets anymore.

Antigravity Machine

My brother built a potent antigravity machine.
It runs on electricity and high-test gasoline.
He sat in it and turned it on and shot up to the ceiling,
which took him by surprise and has him clamoring and squealing.
He's yelling like a maniac and pounding his device.
He's calling it some epithets I think are not too nice.
I guess he should have given just a little more attention
to all the knobs and switches that he put on his invention.
Without a switch to turn it off, he's stuck up there, alas,
until the batteries are dead and it runs out of gas.

The World's Fastest Bicycle

My bicycle's the fastest
that the world has ever seen;
it has supersonic engines
and a flame-retardant sheen.

My bicycle will travel
a gazillion miles an hour.
It has rockets on the handlebars
for supplemental power.

The pedals both are jet-propelled
to help you pedal faster,
and the shifter is equipped
with an electric turboblaster.

The fender has a parachute
in case you need to brake.
Yes, my bike is undeniably
the fastest one they make.

My bicycle's incredible!
I love the way it feels,
and I'll like it even more
when Dad removes the training wheels!

My Dad's a Secret Agent

My dad's a secret agent.
He's an undercover spy.
He's the world's best detective.
He's the perfect private eye.

He's a Pinkerton, a gumshoe.
He's a snoop and he's a sleuth.
He's unrivaled at detecting
and uncovering the truth.

He's got eyesight like an eagle.
He's got hearing like a bat.
He can outsmell any bloodhound.
He's as stealthy as a cat.

He can locate nearly anything
with elementary ease.
But no matter how he looks and looks,
my dad can't find his keys.

34

Swimming Ool

Swimming in the swimming pool
is where I like to "B,"
wearing underwater goggles
so that I can "C."
Yesterday, before I swam,
I drank a cup of "T."
Now the pool is just an "ool"
because I took a "P."

I Went to the Doctor

I went to the doctor,
all covered in bumps.
He said, "You've got chickenpox,
measles, and mumps."

He said, "You've got whooping cough,
tetanus, rubella,
digestive dysfunction
from green salmonella.

"You're covered with head lice,
mosquitoes, and fleas.
You've even got pinkeye
and mad cow disease.

"What's more, you've got cooties,
a cold, and the flu,
but don't be upset;
I know just what to do."

He told me, "I promise
this won't hurt a bit,"
then grabbed a syringe
like a barbecue spit.

He made me bend over
the seat of my chair,
then plunged that big needle
in my you-know-where.

So now I'm all cured
of my cooties and fleas,
my whooping cough, measles,
and mad cow disease.

He cured me of every last
sniffle and bump,
and now I'm all better—
except for my rump.

I Slipped on a Banana Peel

I slipped on a banana peel
and fell and hit my head.
I slipped upon a patch of ice,
which nearly killed me dead.

I slipped upon a roller skate
and tumbled into space.
I slipped inside the bathtub,
and I landed on my face.

I slipped upon the basement stairs
and on the kitchen floor.
I wish that I could stop myself
from slipping anymore.

So now I only wear my shoes
or boots or clogs or flippers,
but I don't want to slip again,
so I don't wear my slippers.

My Personal Slave

I'm making my brother my personal slave,
so now when I greet you, my brother will wave.
He'll do all my homework; he'll take all my tests.
He'll clean up my messes and wait on my guests.

He'll hold out my hanky whenever I sneeze.
He'll say that *he* did it if I "cut the cheese."
He'll go take a bath if I play in the dirt.
He'll eat all my spinach then feed me dessert.

He'll empty the garbage and vacuum the floors
and finish my other unsavory chores,
like washing the dishes and mowing the yard
or anything else even modestly hard.

I really enjoy all the effort I save
by making my brother my personal slave.
And though I'll admit how exciting it is,
I'm not sure it's worth it, 'cause next week I'm his.

Talented Family

My family's very talented;
I'm certain you'll agree.
We each possess a special skill
that anyone can see.

My brother's good at burying
his finger up his nose.
My sister's good at covering
her room with dirty clothes.

My father's good at eating soup
in big, disgusting slurps.
My mother's good at cutting loose
with record-breaking burps.

Our dog is good at piddling
in the back seat of the car.
The baby's good at putting
Pop-Tarts in the VCR.

Myself, I'm good at sleeping late
and making lots of noise
and cluttering the living room
with comic books and toys.

So though we're very talented,
I'm sad to say it's true:
We're only good at doing things
we're not supposed to do.

My Sister's Name Is "Seven"

My sister's name is "Seven,"
and my brother's name is "Eight."
My parents gave them freaky names
I'm sure they thought were great.

They could have named him "Michael,"
and they could have named her "Sue."
Instead they both decided that
no normal names would do.

My brother could be "Brandon."
Maybe "Benjamin" or "Bill."
They could have named him "William"
and then simply called him "Will."

My sister could be "Sarah."
Maybe "Kimberly" or "Kelsey."
They could have named her "Caroline"
or "Katherine" or "Chelsea."

My brother could be "Steven,"
or they could have named him "Todd."
Instead his name is even,
and my sister's name is odd.

Valentine's Day Card

I'd rather fight a tiger, covered head-to-toe in gravy.
I'd rather spend a decade scrubbing toilets in the navy.
I'd rather hug a porcupine; I'd rather wrestle eels.
I'd rather run a marathon with splinters in my heels.
I'd rather sleep on mattresses of razorblades and nails.
I'd rather try to skinny-dip with starving killer whales.
I'd rather be tormented by a gang of angry punks.
I'd rather share a bedroom with a family of skunks.

I'd rather dine on Brussels sprouts and spinach for a year.
I'd rather ride a camel race with blisters on my rear.
I'd rather eat a half a ton of liverwurst and lard
than say how much I like you in this Valentine's Day card.

Vacation Frustration

Our family vacationed in Europe.
We flew to the beaches of Spain.
We hopped on a ferry to England.
We traveled through France on a train.

We lugged all our luggage to Denmark.
We dragged all our baggage to Greece.
We hoisted our backpacks and handbags,
our suitcase, our trunk, and valise.

We rambled through dozens of ruins.
We wandered through castles galore.
We must have seen hundreds of statues—
cathedrals and mosques by the score.

We pored over paintings in Paris.
We tramped through museums in Rome.
And all of the while I was thinking
how much I would rather be home.

At last we are done with our travels.
We've seen every kingdom and nation.
But we're so completely exhausted
that we need another vacation!

No More Water

Both my parents told me not to,
but I did it anyway.
Now our water tank is empty,
and the well ran dry today.

Not a drop is in the reservoir.
The lake's completely dry.
Everybody's getting thirstier,
and I'm the reason why.

All the rivers are depleted.
All the streams no longer flow.
All the seas and all the oceans
are devoid of H_2O.

No, there isn't any water,
not a drop is left to drink,
'cause I left the faucet running,
and it all went down the sink.

I Dreamed That I Was Flying

I dreamed that I was in my room
when much to my surprise,
I found that if I flapped my arms
it made me start to rise.

I waved my arms a little more
and floated off the ground.
I rose up to the ceiling,
and I had a look around.

I flapped around my bedroom
then decided what I'd do:
I opened up my window,
waved my arms, and out I flew!

I flew around the city
with surprising grace and ease.
I sailed along the rooftops,
and I soared among the trees.

I chased a pair of pigeons
'round the playground in the park.
I raced beside a robin
and cavorted with a lark.

And when I tired of flying
and decided I should rest,
I joined a sleeping eagle
for a nap inside his nest.

I woke confused this morning,
and I had to scratch my head,
for underneath my covers
I found feathers in my bed!

Lousy Catcher's Mitt

I bought myself a catcher's mitt
so I could catch a ball.
But all I ever caught were things
I didn't want at all.

I caught a fish, I caught a cab;
just how I can't explain.
I caught my brother telling lies.
I even caught a train.

I caught a show, I caught a crook,
I caught the evening news.
I caught my sister kissing boys,
and then I caught a snooze.

Come see my lousy catcher's mitt—
a wonder to behold!
I've never caught a single ball,
and now I've caught a cold!

I'b God a Code

"I'b sick," I pout ad blow my doze.
"I'b misseeg all by favorite shows.
I hab to stay id bed, you see.
My mob wode led me watch TB.
She breegs me chicked soup ad says
that I should try to get sub rest.
Bud I'b too bored ad icky feeleeg,
tired of stareeg ad the ceileeg,
achy, cougheeg, stuffed up, too.
Bud thaks for askeeg. How are you?"

My Excuse

This morning I was walking
past the local county jail
when I was captured by a pirate
just released on bail.
He took me to his pirate ship
and taught me how to sail
and made me wed his daughter,
who was covered by a veil.
We sailed the seven stormy seas
through hurricane and gale,
but while we were marauding,
we were swallowed by a whale.
We soon escaped by torturing
the whale with a nail

and floating to the shoreline
in an empty wooden pail.
An Indian then guided us
along a western trail
and led us to a stagecoach
that was carrying the mail.
We all delivered letters
through the sleet and snow and hail,
until we found a train,
and then we rode upon the rail.
I barely made it back to school
to tell you of my tale.
I'm sorry that I missed the test;
I hope I didn't fail!

U.S. MAIL

There's a Witch outside My Window

There's a witch outside my window,
and she will not go away.
There's a gremlin on my doorstep,
and I think he's there to stay.

There's a troll demanding candy
and a mummy wanting sweets.
There's a ghost, a ghoul, a goblin,
and they're clamoring for treats.

And as if that weren't enough
to be considered rather shocking,
a vampire rang my doorbell,
and the bogeyman is knocking.

My abode is now surrounded
by the recently deceased.
They're in search of gum and chocolate
on which they plan to feast.

It's the strangest situation
that I think I've ever seen.
How I wish they'd go away
and just come back on Halloween.

The Horsemen Are Headless
This Evening

The horsemen are headless this evening.
The werewolves are howling and hairy.
The mummies are rising from out of their crypts.
The vampires are equally scary.

The trolls are pugnacious and plodding.
The goblins are grinning and green.
The ogres are rabid and running amok.
The ghosts can just barely be seen.

The banshees are wailing and moaning.
The zombies are dragging their feet,
and gremlins engaging in mischievous fun
are dancing around in the street.

With such evil creatures abounding,
I don't know what I'm gonna do,
'cause Mom made my Halloween costume this year
and dressed me as Winnie-the-Pooh.

HONEY

Itches

I'm covered in calamine lotion
from forehead on down to my feeters
to stop me from scratching the itches
of hundreds of bites from mosqueeters.

My arms and my legs are so itchy,
they feel like they're starting to smoke.
I guess that I got that from playing
in patches of red poison oak.

As if it could not be more painful,
my stomach is rashy and hivey,
my back and my sides are all blotchy
from wandering through poison ivy.

Despite that I'm itching like crazy,
I hardly can wait until when
my itches and rashes are better,
so I can go camping again.

Spinach Is One of My Favorite Foods

Oh, spinach is one of my favorite foods;
I savor each wonderful bite.
I eat it each day
served up every which way.
I also enjoy it at night.

And yes, I like sauerkraut, turnips, and leeks,
and all kinds of peppers and shoots.
I think that the beet
is just perfect to eat,
like all other vegetable roots.

I love every leaf, every seed, every sprout,
each plant in the vegetable phylum.
I like to consume
them right here in my room
at the lunatic mental asylum.

Big Lunch

I started arranging my alphabet soup,
concocting big words to devour.
I swallowed a B U I L D I N G.
I gobbled a S T R E E T,
and then I ingested a T O W E R.

I snacked on a S U B W A Y.
I bolted a B U S.
I wolfed down a P A S S E N G E R T R A I N.
I chewed up M O N T A N A.
I gulped I N D I A N A,
then tossed down the whole S T A T E O F M A I N E.

I ate the G R A N D C A N Y O N.
I lunched on the R O C K I E S,
and A S I A, I slurped from my cup.
I would have been fine,
but I started to dine
on M Y H O M E W O R K,
and then I threw up.

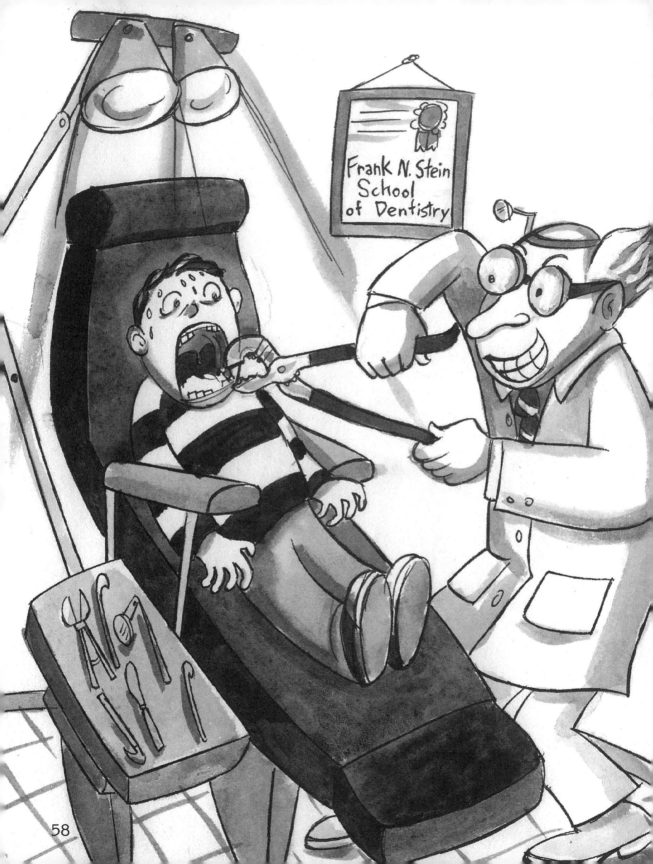

58

The Dentist Pulled My Tooth Out

The dentist pulled my tooth out,
and he thought it was such fun,
he grabbed his pliers
and dental priers
and pulled another one.

"Yippee! Hooray! What awesome fun!"
he shouted out with glee.
He grinned a grin
then went back in
and pulled out number three.

Then number four and number five
and numbers six and seven
were followed by
a cheerful cry
of "Eight! Nine! Ten! Eleven!"

He took a few more from the top
and some from underneath;
he yanked them fast
until at last
he'd pulled out all my teeth.

Without my teeth I cannot chew;
I just eat soup and mush.
But don't be sad.
I'm kind of glad—
I'll never have to brush!

Hitting Rules

My brother isn't very nice,
he's cruel as can be,
and so my parents made some rules
to stop him hitting me.
He's not supposed to wallop me.
He cannot punch or whack.
He must not slap, tap, beat, prod, poke,
nor slam, strike, knock, thump, crack.
My parents made so many rules
to try to stop his fighting.
I wish they'd make just one more rule
preventing him from biting.

My Special Diet

Fish sticks, Tator Tots,
candy bars, baloney.
Ice cream, bubble gum,
cheesy macaroni.
This is all I ever eat.
Don't knock it 'til you try.
I haven't lost a single pound,
but still I love my diet.

The Sad Story of Tommy McTivver

Sit back and I'll tell you of Tommy McTivver,
whose parents so cruelly made him eat liver.
I'll try to explain in a sensitive way
why Tommy McTivver is not here today.

You see, when you serve up that rubbery meat,
it smells like the sweatsocks of stinky old feet.
The room becomes filled with the hideous odor
of all the manure in the state of Dakota.

Poor Tommy was given a plateful of liver,
which frightened the dog and which made the cat shiver.
But nevertheless Tommy did what was right;
he cut a big piece, and he chewed up a bite.

Then what happened next is too horrid to tell;
his body went stiff, and he shrieked as he fell.
The ambulance came, and they drove him away
and promised to have him returned in a day.

The driver, however, drove right off the street
when he heard what Tommy had happened to eat.
The man accidentally drove into the river,
and all because Tommy McTivver ate liver.

So everyone died, and I'm sorry to say,
this story could happen again here today.
So please, Mom and Dad, think of Tommy McTivver
and don't make me eat one more bite of this liver.

Sick Fish

The fish in our aquarium
are looking rather ill,
and most of them have started
turning green around the gill.

I might have fed them too much food,
forgot to clean their tank,
or maybe they're allergic to
the toys and junk I sank.

Perhaps I broke the thermostat.
I could have cut their air.
What's certain is they're sickly
from my utter lack of care.

But even though they're looking ill
I still have cause to gloat;
they're obviously talented—
they're learning how to float!

Fancy Dancer

The fanciest dancer
who ever did dance
was Elmo Fernando
Rodrigo McGants.
McGants did a dance
that was twenty parts tango,
eleven parts polka,
and five parts fandango,
with thirty parts two-stepping
jitterbug waltz,
a tap dance, a back flip,
and four somersaults.
He spun like a top
for a hundred rotations,
then swung and lambada'd
with pelvic gyrations.
He rhumba'd, he mamboed,
he boogied to disco;
he did the merengue
from Boston to Frisco.
He limboed and cha-cha'd
from China to France,
completing the world's
most intricate dance,
and all because someone
put ants in the pants
of Elmo Fernando
Rodrigo McGants.

Don't Bring Camels in the Classroom

Don't bring camels in the classroom.
Don't bring scorpions to school.
Don't bring rhinos, rats, or reindeer.
Don't bring mice or moose or mule.

Pull your penguin off the playground.
Put your python in a tree.
Place your platypus wherever
you think platypi should be.

Lose your leopard and your lemur.
Leave your llama and your leech.
Take your tiger, toad, and toucan
anywhere but where they teach.

Send your wombat and your weasel
with your wasp and wolverine.
Hide your hedgehog and hyena
where you're sure they won't be seen.

Please get rid of your gorilla.
Please kick out your kangaroo.
No, the teacher didn't mean it
when she called the class a "zoo."

teacher

Merlo the Magnificent

I am Merlo the Magnificent.
I'm skilled at sleight of hand.
I'm a master prestidigitator—
greatest in the land.

Yes, at making things invisible
I'm truly the premier.
There is nothing that I cannot make
completely disappear.

I have hidden doves and rabbits
in the lining of my cloak.
I've concealed my stage assistant
in a camouflage of smoke.

I've evaporated elephants,
put tigers out of view.
I've disguised the Eiffel Tower
and the Wall of China, too.

I have made a mountain vanish
and an ocean fade from sight.
I've eclipsed the midday sun
to turn the afternoon to night.

I'm undoubtedly the best
at getting things to disappear,
so would someone please explain this to me:
Why are you still here?

Magician

I'm learning to be a magician.
I'm conjuring magical spells,
performing complex incantations
with all kinds of whistles and bells.

I'm practicing several new card tricks.
I've learned how to juggle with rings.
I know how to levitate tables
and other inanimate things.

A rabbit will leap from my top hat.
A dove will fly out of my sleeve.
I'll mystify all of the skeptics
and even make cynics believe.

So come watch an elephant vanish.
I'll show you a trick with some ropes.
For this is my lifelong ambition
and these are my greatest of hopes:

I hope I can startle my viewers.
I hope I can muster a laugh.
But mostly I hope that my sister
allows me to saw her in half.

New Computer

We have bought a new computer
that's the fastest ever seen.
It has terabytes of mem'ry
and a forty-eight-inch screen.

It has all the latest gizmos
and accessories galore.
It has every last peripheral
they carried at the store.

It has disk drives by the dozen,
it has twenty-seven mice,
and it even has a microwave
included in the price.

It can teach you how to mambo.
It can play the violin.
It can calculate the distance
from Botswana to Berlin.

MOVE A5
ROOK TO A3

It can speak in seven languages
with scholarly finesse,
then defeat the world's grandmasters
in a tournament of chess.

It can conjure antigravity
or build a time machine.
Our computer is undoubtedly
the fastest ever seen.

When we went and bought it yesterday,
we thought it pretty neat,
but today our new computer
is already obsolete.

Double Danny

My name is Double Danny, and
I always do things twice.
I'm completely double-jointed,
and I'm double doggone nice.

When I see a double feature,
I prefer to double-date.
I arrive there double early,
and I leave there double late.

I like words with double meanings.
I like doing double takes.
I wear double-breasted jackets
and eat double-layered cakes.

When it comes to doing homework, though,
I'm not a double dunce.
For I've got a double standard,
and I only do it once.

Stumblebum Stan

I'm Stumblebum Stan, the Invisible Man.
How I love to draw pictures and paint.
I sell every sketch, and the money they fetch
is so much you would probably faint.

I'm rather surprised that my art is so prized,
and I laugh all the way to the bank.
All the pictures I draw are exactly alike
because all I can draw is a blank.

What to Remember in School

Forget that two times four is eight.
Forget the name of every state.
Forget the answers on the test.
Forget which way is east or west.

Forget the myths of ancient Rome.
Forget to bring your books from home.
Forget the words you learned to spell.
Forget to hear the recess bell.

Forget your homeroom teacher's name.
Forget the after-school game.
Forget which team's supposed to win.
Forget to turn your homework in.

Forget the distance to the moon.
Forget how many days in June.
Forget the capital of France.
But *don't* forget to wear your pants!

December 26

A BB gun.
A model plane.
A basketball.
A 'lectric train.
A bicycle.
A cowboy hat.
A comic book.
A baseball bat.
A deck of cards.
A science kit.
A racing car.
A catcher's mitt.
So that's my list
of everything
that Santa Claus
forgot to bring.

Dear Santa Claus

I don't believe in Santa Claus
like many other folks.
I think you're just a fairy tale.
I think you're just a hoax.

I don't believe you're keeping track
of who's been bad or good.
I don't believe you know if I've
been sleeping when I should.

I don't believe that reindeer fly.
I don't believe in elves.
I think the toys beneath our tree
were bought from toy-store shelves.

I once believed (when I was six);
at seven I know better.
But if I'm wrong and you exist,
please disregard this letter.

77

Don't Rat on a Mouse

Don't badger a groundhog.
Don't crow at a grouse.
Don't hound a Chihuahua.
Don't rat on a mouse.

Don't parrot a peacock.
Don't buffalo moose.
Don't bat at a squirrel.
Don't duck from a goose.

Don't slug caterpillars.
Don't leech off of worms.
Don't fly at mosquitoes.
Don't bug any germs.

Don't crab at a lobster.
Don't tick off a louse.
Don't ape a gorilla.
Don't rat on a mouse.

Just take some advice
and remember this clue:
If you leave them alone,
they won't monkey with you.

Things You Don't Need to Know

Don't test a rattlesnake's rattle.
Don't count the teeth of a shark.
Don't stick your head in the mouth of a bulldog
to find out what's making him bark.

Don't count the stripes on a tiger.
Don't squeeze an elephant's trunk.
Don't pet the scales of a boa constrictor
and don't lift the tail of a skunk.

Don't study spots on a leopard.
Don't check the charge of an eel.
Don't pull the claws on a grizzly bear's paws,
regardless of how brave you feel.

Don't pull a porcupine's whiskers.
Don't touch a crocodile's toe.
Learn all you like, but try not to forget:
There are some things you don't need to know.

The Cow Town Ballet

This here is the story of Jed Beaudelay,
who once was the head of the Cow Town Ballet,
the greatest of all of the old western sights,
for Jed would take milk cows and dress them in tights.

In tutus and slippers his cows would sashay;
they'd spin pirouettes, they'd glissade and plié.
And cowpokes from Boston to Monterey Bay
would journey to Cow Town to see the ballet.

And every night how his cattle would dance!
They'd act out a musical cattle romance.
With skill and precision, with grace and with flair,
they'd glide 'cross the stage and they'd leap through the air.

And when it was over the cowpokes would cheer,
and even the manliest men shed a tear,
for nowhere on earth but the Cow Town Ballet
had anyone ever seen cattle sashay.

Old Jed Beaudelay would still run the ballet,
if not for the fact that when cattle sashay
and all of their tutus are flapping around,
their costumes make sort of a shuffling sound.

And some no-good cowpoke, on hearing that sound,
grew rather unhappy. He stopped and he frowned,
then ran to the sheriff, deciding to tattle.
So Jed was arrested for rustling cattle.

Benson Baxter

With a basketball, a bowling ball,
and baseball bat he came.
He had golf clubs, cleats, and catcher's mitts
to help him in the game.

He had Rollerblades and elbow pads
with climbing ropes and straps,
plus athletic shorts and running shoes
to race a couple laps.

He was schlepping all his scuba gear,
his snorkel, and his mask.
He had suitable accessories
for nearly any task.

He had helmets, hats, and headgear.
He had uniforms galore.
Why, he even brought the costume
of a Spanish matador.

But though Benson Baxter came prepared
for almost every sport,
he forgot his tennis racquet,
so they threw him off the court.

Levitating Lester

I am Levitating Lester.
I am lighter than a feather.
I'm as buoyant as a bubble.
I am weightless altogether.

If you carefully observe me,
you will see me floating soon.
I will rise up from my mattress
like a helium balloon.

Yes, it happens every morning:
I awaken in my bed,
and I drift up to the ceiling,
where I sometimes bump my head.

If I wake before the sunrise,
it's a miserable flight,
for I cannot see the ceiling
when there isn't any light.

So I always keep a flashlight
on my bed where I recline,
so in case I wake in darkness,
I can simply rise and shine.

Zzzzz

I see zebras from Zimbabwe
zipping all around the zoo.
I see Zeus up in the zodiac,
a zillion zithers, too.

There are zephyrs blowing zeppelins
that are zooming near and far.
There are zealots counting zeroes
in a zone near Zanzibar.

There are Zulus wearing zoot suits,
eating zwieback and zucchini,
plus a zombie with a zipper
on his zinnia bikini.

Yes, I always have the zaniest,
most zonked-out dreams like these,
because every time I go to sleep
I try to catch some Zs.

Index

Also from Meadowbrook Press

✦ *If Pigs Could Fly . . .*
Bruce Lansky is back with a second serving of rip-roaring, side-splitting, rolling-on-the-floor poems about smelly diapers, chubby relatives, toothless grandmas, dirty socks, impolite dogs, burping babies, bad hair days, and more. (Ages 6–12)

✦ *My Dog Ate My Homework!*
Bruce Lansky, the "King of Giggle Poetry," had the help of more than 1,000 students and their teachers in choosing the funniest poems about parents who won't let their kids watch TV, yucky school lunches, and dogs that "water" the flowers. Formerly titled *Poetry Party*. (Ages 6–12)

✦ *Kids Pick the Funniest Poems*
Three hundred kids will tell you that this book contains the funniest poems for kids— because they picked them! They chose the funniest poems by Jeff Moss, Shel Silverstein, Jack Prelutsky, and Bruce Lansky. This book is guaranteed to please children ages 6–12!

✦ *No More Homework! No More Tests!*
This is the funniest collection of poems about school by the most popular children's poets, including Shel Silverstein, Jack Prelutsky, Bruce Lansky, David L. Harrison, Colin McNaughton, Kalli Dakos, and others who know how to find humor in any subject. (Ages 6–12)

✦ *A Bad Case of the Giggles*
Bruce Lansky knows that nothing motivates children to read poetry more than a poem that makes them laugh. That's why this book will turn your kids into poetry lovers. Every poem in this book had to pass the giggle test of 600 school children. (Ages 6–12)

✦ *Miles of Smiles*
Miles of Smiles features the funniest poems by the most popular children's poets, including Shel Silverstein, Jack Prelutsky, Jeff Moss, Colin McNaughton, David Harrison, Bruce Lansky, and more. (Ages 6–12)

We offer many more titles written to delight, inform, and entertain.
To order books with a credit card or browse our full
selection of titles, visit our web site at:

www.meadowbrookpress.com

or call toll-free to place an order, request a free catalog, or ask a question:

1-800-338-2232

Meadowbrook Press • 5451 Smetana Dive • Minnetonka, MN • 55343

For more poetry fun, visit

www.gigglepoetry.com